What the Foresight

Copyright © 2016 by Alida Draudt and Julia Rose West
All rights reserved.

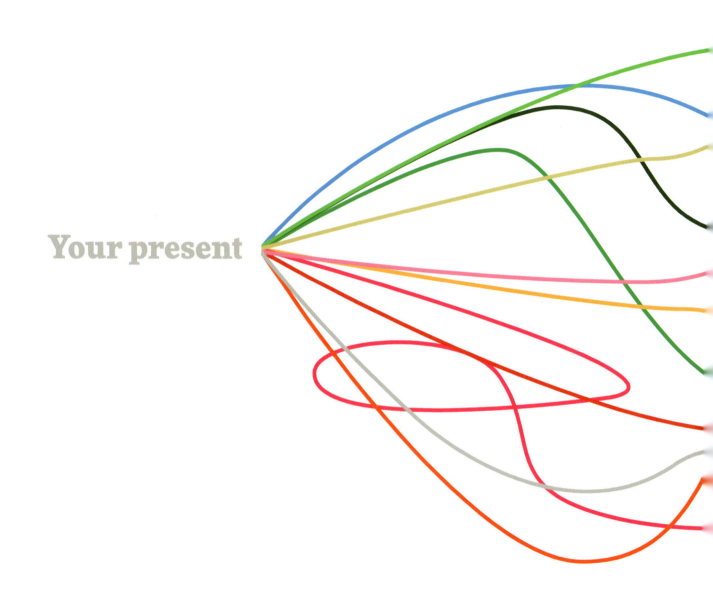

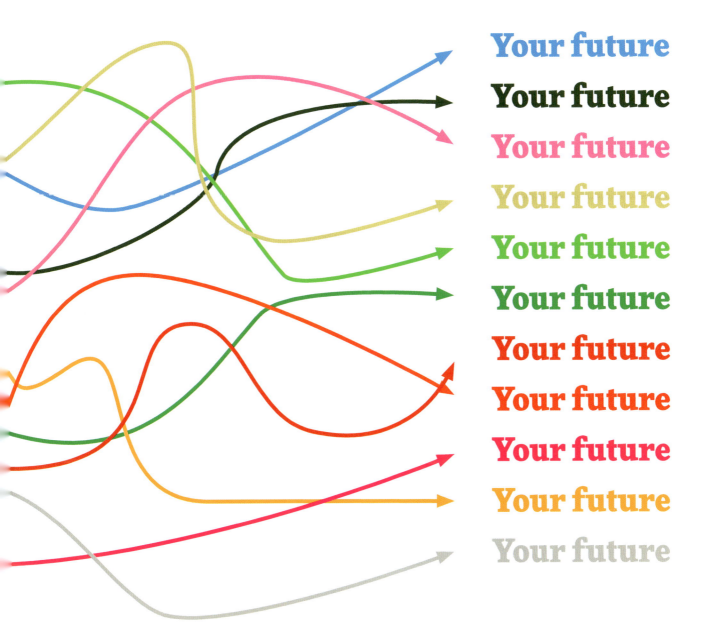

[You have multiple potential futures, not just one.]

A transformational workbook helping you explore your personal futures to make them more tangible than before.

"

Change is hard but stagnation is fatal.
- *Dr. Peter Bishop*

This book is a space to explore your individual futures. We encourage you to share your findings with those closest to you, as only they can best challenge your assumptions you have about your futures. The process begins with you!

These futures and this workbook belongs to:

[Your name here]

This book is dedicated to *all* aspirational futurists. Those who think about their future and seek the tools to do it better.

Not without you

Foresight is a uniquely collaborative discipline, and we want to take this opportunity to thank the community we have had the pleasure of working with and learning from. A huge thank you to the following people for teaching us a variety of foresight tools and techniques, for your direction, thoughtful insights, and most of all for your brutal feedback. This book would not be possible without your help and guidance.

Like any process interpretation, *What the Foresight* has been heavily influenced by thought leaders in the field of foresight and futurism. **Jake Dunagan, Leland Shupp, Brian David Johnson, Chris Arkenberg, and Matthew Manos** have introduced us to the facets of strategic foresight and a breadth of application potential. **Stuart Candy, Ari Popper, Betty Sue Flowers, Andy Hines, Wendy Schultz, and James Dator** have been inspirations throughout our continued learning process. Particular thanks to **Peter Bishop** and **Sara Skvirsky** for unparalleled assistance and advice during the creation of this workbook. Finally, thank you to our fellow **California College of the Arts DMBA colleagues** for challenging, questioning, collaborating, and supporting us through this process.

Many more within the foresight community have had a part in our education and application of expanding the foresight toolkit. Even more practitioners create inspirational, impactful, and innovative work across an enormous breadth of industries. We thank you.

"We all think about the future we just don't do it very well."
- Jake Dunagan

Contents

This book will...
PAGE 06

Why foresight
PAGE 10

What foresight is
PAGE 14

Workbook!
PAGE 20

Warm-up to Your Futures 22
Values Discovery 26
Surfacing Assumptions 36
Other Futures 44
Backcasting 64
Implications 72
Reflection 78

What to do next
PAGE 82

Back of the book stuff
PAGE 86

Extras
PAGE 94

CHAPTER ONE

This book will…

ABOUT THIS CHAPTER

A glimpse into what this book has in store for you.

This book is for those who haven't figured it all out, don't know what exactly they want, or what they should avoid - it's for everyone.

We'd like to begin by introducing you to two illustrative characters:

Harper has always loved art, dreaming since college of living in San Francisco while working for an agency as a professional designer. He has envisioned this life often while working on his art from a small dedicated space in his apartment, however Harper hasn't made an effort to map out how he would make his dream a reality. While he has taken the obvious steps, including a Bachelors in Art and Design and an internship, for various reasons he never quite made his professional goals happen. Harper figured that his dream would manifest itself, subsequently not taking the time to envision his preferred future or consider other possible futures. On the eve of his ten-year high school class reunion, he finds himself bartending in his college town, reflecting on how different the past years could have been if only he had exerted a more concerted and mindful effort…

Driving home from visiting her newborn grandson, Cindy passes the dark windows of the office building where she spent the last twenty five years. She always envisioned retiring with her husband to a small coastal town, enjoying walks from their cozy bungalow – but so much has changed since her husband's untimely passing. Now she finds herself reconsidering what she wants to do with her time. Financial changes and the birth of her first grandson have made her realize she will not be relocating any time soon. She now feels perplexed when thinking about what her future will entail.

Throughout this workbook we will explore various avenues and tools utilized in foresight. Strategic foresight was first markedly utilized in World War II as a strategic tactic. Scenario planning subsequently caught the attention of corporations, notable early adopters being Royal Dutch Shell starting in the 1970s, followed shortly thereafter by Xerox and American Express. Global Business Network popularized the practice into a field that is still growing toward wide utilization. This book gives you a glimpse at a few tools to guide your personal foresight practice.

This workbook will help you better think about your futures by teaching you how to apply the discipline of strategic foresight to your personal life.

We created this book to help you better think about your futures. Not only is it fun to think about what might be, but conscious consideration about futures helps you better understand your present.

You might be asking, *"how does that work"*? Thinking about futures can help you see the gap between what you are doing and what you would like to be doing. The ability to see this gap will help you take action toward closing it in order to realize your preferred future rather than waiting for it to happen.

"What the Foresight" is not a deep dive into the world of strategic foresight and futures thinking. It's more like a guided snorkel. We believe foresight is not for a select few but rather a way of thinking that everyone can learn given the right mindset. This book provides an overview of guiding principles in strategic foresight. The goal is for you to explore your personal future options using the tools of strategic foresight. To do that, we've taken several tools and distilled them to their core for easy application.

This book is more participatory than passive, more guiding than leading, and more interpretive than prescriptive. We can't make your futures for you, but we can help you think about them in a way you may not have before.

We hope our passion for this subject helps you explore paths unknown in a way that is equally fun and informative.

WHY FUTURES VERSUS A FUTURE

The future can not be predicted. As such, we aim to help you explore a variety of futures so that you can be better prepared for many outcomes. In this book, we will refer to the future as futures — you have multiple possible futures, not just one.

CHAPTER TWO

Why foresight

ABOUT THIS CHAPTER

Positive assessment of futures opens up a spectrum of possibilities you never may have considered but are eager to explore.

Thinking about the future better informs decisions you make in the present.
- Leland Shupp

Sometimes the present feels like a series of actions done because they are familiar, easy, and require little thought. For example, we might take a particular bus to work because we did so yesterday. We're pretty sure it's the fastest route, and why bother to try something different? But what if we told you one potential transit future has no buses? What would be your routine then?

We aren't saying you should stop taking the bus. This is just a way of introducing the power of imagination and creativity. Your futures might hold something very different than your present. By only focusing on today, or worse yet using your past to model your future, you may miss other opportunities waiting for you.

The very idea of thinking about futures can be daunting. It is difficult to think about your life as different than it is today, but it's worth a try. Pushing yourself to think about a variety of futures may help unlock unacknowledged desires, define a preferred path, and navigate around futures you would like to avoid. Even if the futures you consider are completely wacky, that's okay! In a few chapters, you will be exploring and actively designing a variety of personal futures. Consideration of many options helps you focus on what it is that most resonates.

In thinking about your futures, you gain a better grasp on what it means to be you – today and many years from now.

Looking at a variety of futures helps you strategize and plan for your personal future...

The first tenant of foresight is that foresight is not prediction. There is no way to know a singular future, because there is no one future. Your future was not written for you at birth. Rather, your future is a combination of choosing your own adventure and going where the current takes you. You can choose to ignore what may come, not examining future possibilities; this course of inaction, however, will only allow you to be a bystander of your own life rather than the driver of it. Why not embrace your futures and begin examining all possibilities? We will do just that in the workbook section of this book.

We know that life progresses. What this book will help uncover is that there are many routes! So how might you better navigate your prospective options? From challenging to optimistic, fringe to mainstream, an exploration of different futures scenarios will help you question your assumptions about what the future "must" or "will" look like.

Later on in the workbook section, you will begin by going wide – exploring your values and defining assumptions you have about your "future." You will need to be open to many possibilities before you can begin to focus in on your ideal future. Go broad in order to challenge and inspire yourself. Once corners are explored, nooks and crannies revealed, then start to focus. This activity of exploration into many possibilities will help you identify where you truly want to target, and, more importantly, what you want to avoid. Armed with this knowledge, the process of examining your personal futures becomes palpable.

...which empowers you to create your future, not be a passive participant.

Knowing where to aim and what to avoid is a pretty great skill! Examining your futures is step one towards honing that skill; it is just the beginning.

Foresight is a blend of creativity and rigor. A futures mindset allows you to articulate long-term goals and provides you with the knowhow for agile adjustment when change occurs. Part of foresight is visioning. The other is taking action toward that vision; this is the hard part.

While you may design the most amazing future visions for yourself, somewhere along the road your vision will be forced to change. Either from internal or external factors - or both.

The objective of foresight is to create engagement between you and your futures, continuously. Being an active participant may mean frequent reassessment to see if the vision you created still aligns.

Changing circumstances may result in scrapping your vision and reassessing or shifting your strategy. The goal is not to hand you a map and say "proceed"; the goal is to give you the agency to participate in the development of your futures rather than being a passive observer of their creation.

Looking at the big picture can help you to leapfrog and take greater, less risky risk

Imagine you are on a forest slope looking down into a river basin. To cross the river, you can climb down the visibly steep slope, forge the river, and emerge on the opposite bank in an hour or so. Or, you can use a zipline tied to a nearby tree, getting you there in far less time. While the first option is longer, it may be safer, and you know the way. The zipline, on the other hand, is unfamiliar and risky but could be much more efficient. Which do you choose?

The balance of risk in foresight is a delicate one. In order to know whether to use the zipline in the previous scenario, understanding the larger context would be of great benefit. Is the zipline functioning and secure? Is it made of high quality materials and regularly maintained? Answers to these questions and others will add context to your decision and help minimize your risk. Contextual questions surrounding futures scenarios may include: What skills do I possess or will have to gain to make this a reality? What are external factors (see p. 18) that might impact this scenario? Who else might be impacted by or involved in my decisions?

While foresight is about looking out toward potential futures, those futures only make sense within a larger context. Which preferred future you aim yourself toward and which you choose to avoid may change based on larger contextual shifts. Looking at the bigger picture will help you better understand your options and weigh the risk and reward of each. Big picture thinking also helps to elminate the paralysis of repetition to enable a leap forward.

CHAPTER THREE

What foresight is

ABOUT THIS CHAPTER

Foresight is a discipline, but it is also a mindset, a way of thinking everybody can learn.

Foresight is not prediction

Foresight is a mindset, as well as a set of tools, that help the practitioner examine a wide range of feasible future scenarios. We've covered some reasons why you might want to use foresight for your personal life, but how is it used professionally? Scenarios can hit on a vast array of topics centered around a common theme, like the future of transportation, communication, financial services, or health care for example. Foresight professionals leverage tools and methods of foresight in order to stretch beyond facts of the present *(known knowns)*. The exercise of stretching our minds into potential futures helps us recognize aspects we do not yet know and would like to track *(known unknowns)*. It also opens our minds to the possibility that there are factors we may not currently identify, which may have an impact on us at some point down the line *(unknown unknowns)*.

Strategic foresight is a process of examination and evaluation more than anything else. There is not just one tool, but many in the foresight toolkit. The beginning of a foresight project starts with conducting interviews, scanning trends across a wide variety of sources and industries, gathering patterns and applicable events which may impact your specific field of interest, and analyzing the data to create possible future scenarios. All of these steps have multiple approaches and tools. Just as there is no one master future, there is no one prescriptive way to approach each project.

Foresight work includes a great deal of both individual and collective work. In fact, many practicing futurists say futures work requires collaboration. Foresight is difficult, if not impossible, to do alone or in a vacuum. The goal of professional futurists is to unearth potential futures, which may not have been considered previously. The objective is to question or confirm the trajectory we are on, by exploring options for change. What might be the impacts, effects or consequences of these potential changes? And most importantly, what might that mean for how we should operate today?

As a discipline gaining momentum, foresight is integral to a range of industries. Futurists and foresight professionals work internally at large companies, as independent consultants, as part of future-specific organizations, **within academic institutions, governments, and many other areas. The** authors of this book believe strategic foresight is a way of approaching strategic decision making by taking the long view, rather than searching for immediate short-term solutions.

Let's dive in by looking at a few of the foresight tools, and then we will look at how you can apply them to your personal and professional life.

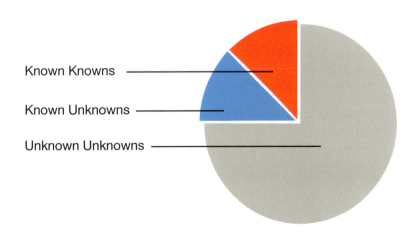

Known Knowns

Known Unknowns

Unknown Unknowns

Graph inspired by Lee Shupp. Unknowns concept, Donald Rumsfeld.

Cone of possibilities

Our world is made up of a vast array of variables, making prediction of one singular future impossible. Instead, we look at a range of possibilities in order to compare and contrast them. The cone of possibilities is one way of visualizing our possible, probable, and preferable futures. This is a conceptual representation that helps futurists and foresight professionals add context to their work.

If you imagine yourself standing in the present, you are at the apex of the cone, your past stretching behind you to the left. The widest, blue cone stretching to the right encompasses all possible futures for consideration. One example of a possible future is that you move to Amsterdam. A stretch for many but possible nonetheless. There are a lot of possibilities out there! These are all the futures that could possibly come to pass, except for unpredictable events in their truest sense, which you never will see coming (sometimes known as Black Swans) until they are part of your present.

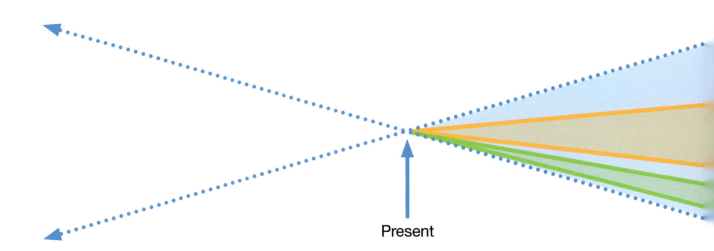

Present

Within the realm of possible is the realm of probable; represented by the yellow cone. ==Probable futures are ones that most likely may happen, given your current trajectory.== The probable cone emanates directly from the apex of today, with some wiggle room. One example of a probable future is that you purchase a home of your own, granted the right opportunities, hard work, and necessary financial means.

==Also within the realm of the possible, but not necessarily within the realm of the probable, is your preferable future.== This is your intentional and desirable future, represented by the green cone. You can see that preferable futures may not proceed directly from your current position at the apex, but instead potentially deviate slightly while staying within the realm of the possible. A preferable future might be that you continually travel for a few years exploring the world.

Below is a simple representation of the cone of possibilities, but imagine what futures might begin to live within the realm of the possible, yet outside of the realms of the probable or preferable! This tool helps you visualize a range of futures, serving as a reminder that every area of the cone of possibilities is at least worth consideration.

Possible Futures - *all options*

Probable Futures - *most likely to happen*

Preferable Futures - *intentional and desirable*

Adapted from Henchey, 1978. Graphic inspired by Dr. Joseph Voros, 2000.

Consider the external with the internal

To use foresight effectively, we need to be aware of how the world at large is changing and how that relates back to ourselves. How will external shifts affect you personally and professionally? This tension is core to the practice of foresight, and is what we mean when we say foresight cannot be done in a vacuum.

Throughout this book you'll be charged with considering what changes may be taking place in the outside world that will influence how you operate. Outside forces might be social, technological, environmental, economic or political.

Let's take the extended drought in California as an example. Temperatures have been rising in the Californian climate creating a decrease in snowfall in the Sierra Nevada mountain range. As California's primary watershed, the Sierra Nevada's lack of precipitation has a direct impact on the amount of water allocated to cities. Let's imagine that to conserve water usage, a mandate has been ordered to decrease the number of showers per week for San Francisco residents. In other words, the rising temperatures and lack of snow are changing San Franciscans' morning routines.

The external world and how it is changing is a key consideration as you move through the exercises found in this book. As you continue, think about what changing factors (social, technological, environmental, economic, and political) may have an influence on you right now and in the future.

WHAT OTHER EXTERNAL FORCES SHOULD BE CONSIDERED?

When considering external forces, take a moment to think about how they may effect your personal futures. For example: **social movements** (e.g. Black Lives Matter, Nuit Debout, LGBTQ civil rights, Farm to Table); **technological advancements** (e.g. virtual and artificial reality, machine learning, proliferation of social media); **politics** (e.g. "Brexit", 2016 U.S. Election, Supreme Court appointments); **environmental changes** (e.g. global climate change); and **economic factors** (e.g. adoption of the Euro, U.S. housing collapse of 2007). How might these forces adjust those factors you expect to stay constant? This is an effective way of checking your assumptions and examining how your futures may unfold - it may be in directions you haven't considered before!

Plausibility

Think back a few pages to the cone of possibilities. Within the possible realm of moving to Amsterdam, both traveling around the world for a year (preferable) and owning your own home (probable) seem like great options, right? While the goal is to imagine a wide variety of possible futures, the idea of plausibility needs to play a role in our process as well. Plausibility is consideration of the believable or realistic. While fun to imagine many far-fetched futures for yourself (first Mars colonist!), to make actionable plans we need to add the layer of plausibility. Is this realistic? Might it be statistically plausible? The plausibility filter is a way of relating external forces to your internal futures.

While it is certainly within the realm of possibility that you move to Amsterdam or become a world traveler for a few years, are these futures plausible? Are they grounded in feasible reality?

The addition of plausibility might seem like a downer, but let's reframe and think of it as an enabler. An enabler of realistic, attainable future possibilities for yourself. By adding a plausible filter to your process of thinking about futures, you focus on futures that can not only be envisioned but attained. That's exciting!

Thinking about plausibility shouldn't limit you from thinking about the extreme or seemingly far-fetched futures. By all means, continue to be innovative about what your possible futures could look like! The plausibility filter is another layer of examination that will help you better understand your futures – to look at them with a discerning eye, an eye toward realization and action.

Time

To envision and create actionable futures for yourself, you need to know what the target is. Time helps you narrow in on that target, a big factor within the foresight discipline. It doesn't matter what time frame you set for yourself - it could be five years, 10 years, even 50 years in the future. What does matter is that you set a time frame before you begin.

Creating time parameters will help focus your futures exploration and give weight to the milestones you set in order to get there. You don't always have to choose the same time frame. In fact, envisioning possible personal futures within a variety of time frames is fun and interesting to play around with.

During the course of this book, and most particularly in the workbook section, you will be prompted to think of certain time periods in order to use the foresight tools. We encourage you to try your hand at making these tools your own, and utilize the extra tear-outs in the back of the book to experiment.

All you need is to define how far in the future you want to explore, and your futures are up to you!

CHAPTER FOUR

Workbook!

ABOUT THIS CHAPTER

A series of seven exercises dedicated to exploring your personal futures using the tools of foresight.

Sometimes progress necessitates discomfort

Imagine you are sitting by a creek, making a paper boat. Your expectation is that you will plop the boat in the water and watch it happily travel downstream. On your first attempt, however, your boat runs aground on a rock, never making it more than three feet from you.

What the boat really needs, you realize, is a method of guidance. Oars, or sails, or some way of controlling its direction and course. You need tools to successfully navigate your intended course.

Most people treat their futures like a paper boat - sailing downstream without any tools to maneuver. This workbook section includes the tools you can use to navigate your personal futures. While they are formatted the same for everyone, just like oars or sails, the way in which you use them make them solely yours.

To help you with this, two personas will be used throughout this section. Harper and Cindy, who we met in chapter one, will serve as guides and examples for how each exercise might be applied to your life.

HARPER, 28

Harper lives in his college town of Madison, Wisconsin. He works as a bartender but dreams of moving to San Francisco to utilize his degree in art and design. Harper has sold art pieces at local farmer's markets and coffee shops, but hasn't made the leap toward becoming a design professional. As his ten-year high school **reunion approaches, he dreads disclosing his current profession to former classmates.**

CINDY, 65

Cindy just turned 65 and is on the verge of making a transition into retirement. As a employee of the medical industry, a mother to three children, and a caretaker to aging parents, Cindy spent the majority of her life looking after others. Welcoming her first grandson into the world has been bittersweet given the passing of her husband last year. While her vision of retirement used to include the two of them in a cozy cottage nestled in a coastal town, Cindy is unsure of her future. Financial insecurity has made her realize staying close to family is a must, and now she finds herself re-evaluating her options.

01.

Warm-up to Your Futures

BENEFIT

Time is our propulsion. Learning to operate within established timelines will help move us towards future possibilities.

01. **Warm-up to Your Futures**
02. Values Discovery
03. Surfacing Assumptions
04. Other Futures
05. Backcasting
06. Implications
07. Reflection

Write your future ages

_____ 2020	_____ 2033	_____ 2046	_____ 2059	_____ 2072
_____ 2021	_____ 2034	_____ 2047	_____ 2060	_____ 2073
_____ 2022	_____ 2035	_____ 2048	_____ 2061	_____ 2074
_____ 2023	_____ 2036	_____ 2049	_____ 2062	_____ 2075
_____ 2024	_____ 2037	_____ 2050	_____ 2063	_____ 2076
_____ 2025	_____ 2038	_____ 2051	_____ 2064	_____ 2077
_____ 2026	_____ 2039	_____ 2052	_____ 2065	_____ 2078
_____ 2027	_____ 2040	_____ 2053	_____ 2066	_____ 2079
_____ 2028	_____ 2041	_____ 2054	_____ 2067	_____ 2080
_____ 2029	_____ 2042	_____ 2055	_____ 2068	_____ 2081
_____ 2030	_____ 2043	_____ 2056	_____ 2069	_____ 2082
_____ 2031	_____ 2044	_____ 2057	_____ 2070	_____ 2083
_____ 2032	_____ 2045	_____ 2058	_____ 2071	_____ 2084

A slight jump forward

Using the previous page, let's look at a few future time intervals. For each interval, write the age you will be. This exercise will help add context when thinking about your future. By articulating your age at certain intervals, our goal is to help make future time periods a bit more tangible and realistic.

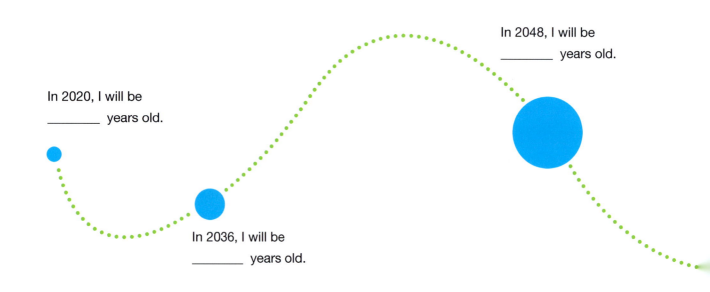

In 2020, I will be _____ years old.

In 2036, I will be _____ years old.

In 2048, I will be _____ years old.

The further out we look, the more possible futures there are – reflected in the increasing size of the circles below.

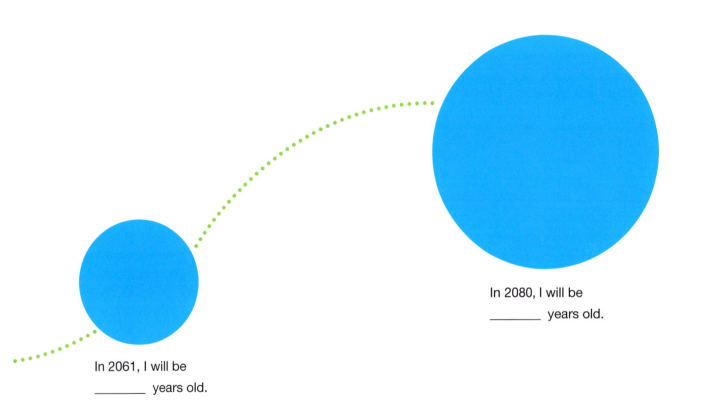

In 2061, I will be _____ years old.

In 2080, I will be _____ years old.

02.

Values Discovery

BENEFIT

Your values are your north star – fully understanding them will help you navigate your futures.

01. Warm-up to Your Futures
02. Values Discovery
03. Surfacing Assumptions
04. Other Futures
05. Backcasting
06. Implications
07. Reflection

Discover your values, letter from your futures, write your obituary

Ever wonder how what you're doing now relates to how you want to be remembered? Yeah, us too. This exercise will help you to get out of your day-to-day life and better imagine your futures. Letters from your futures have a sneaky way of doing that. By imagining your life outside of the present, you can gain clarity towards how you want to live right now.

To the right is one of the obituaries for the singer Lou Reed. Notice how his accomplishments were not overtly mentioned but implied, *"his songs of the pain and beauty in the world will fill many people with the incredible joy he felt for life."* The focus is on his impact and contribution.

Through exploring how you want to be remembered, you are exposing what you value in yourself - what you feel are the true aspects of your character. Understanding your values and what matters to you will help you better craft futures with these values in mind.

On the next few pages, you will write a letter to your granddaughter from your future self, and tweet your obituary. Identify key words and phrases within these two exercises - the stuff that is most compelling and gives you goosebumps. These are your values. In the Lou Reed example, we might imply his values were spirituality, empathy, peace, and beauty. The following page includes a list of values to get you started.

Inspired by ZAG, by Marty Neumeier.

For Lou Reed
October 31, 2013 - 1:15pm

To our neighbors:

What a beautiful fall! Everything shimmering and golden and all that incredible soft light. Water surrounding us.

Lou and I have spent a lot of time here in the past few years, and even though we're city people this is our ==spiritual home.==

Last week I promised Lou to get him out of the hospital and come home to Springs. And we made it!

Lou was a tai chi master and spent his last days here being happy and dazzled ==by the beauty and power and softness of nature.== He died on Sunday morning looking at the trees and doing the famous 21 form of tai chi with just his musician hands moving through the air.

Lou was a prince and a fighter and I know his songs of the ==pain and beauty in the world== will fill many people with the incredible ==joy== he felt for life. Long live the beauty that comes down and through and onto all of us.

Laurie Anderson, his loving wife and eternal friend

Letter to your granddaughter

Write a letter from your future self to your granddaughter. You may want to provide her some advice, or you may want to tell her about your life, your experiences, and your greatest accomplishments. Circle the words that give you goosebumps.

_____

_____

_____

_____

_____

_____

_____

_____

_____

_____

_____

Inspired by Peter Bishop.

Tweet your obituary

Write an obituary for yourself using only 140 characters. Reference the words you circled on the previous page. Try to use those words, or others like them, to write your 140-character obit.

Inspired by Zoe Bezpalko.

List of Common Values

Accountability Accuracy Achievement Adventurous Altruism Ambition Assertiveness Balance Being the best Belonging Boldness Calmness Carefulness Challenge Cheerfulness Clear-mindedness Commitment Community Compassion Competitiveness Consistency Contentment Continuity Contribution Control Cooperation Correctness Courtesy Creativity Curiosity Decisiveness Democratic Dependability Determination Devoutness Diligence Discipline Discretion Diversity Dynamism Economy Effectiveness Efficiency Elegance Empathy Enjoyment Enthusiasm Equality Excellence Excitement Expertise Exploration Expressiveness Fairness Faith Family Fidelity Fitness Fluency Focus Freedom Fun Generosity Goodness Grace Growth Happiness Hard work Health Helping society Holiness Honesty Honor Humility

Improvement Independence Ingenuity Inner harmony Inquisitiveness Insightfulness Intelligence Intellectual status Intuition Joy Justice Kindness Leadership Legacy Love Loyalty Making a difference Mastery Merit Obedience Openness Order Originality Patriotism Perfection Piety Positivity Practicality Preparedness Professionalism Prudence Quality Reliability Resourcefulness Restraint Results-oriented Rigor Security Self-actualization Self-control Selflessness Self-reliance Sensitivity Serenity Service Shrewdness Simplicity Soundness Speed Spontaneity Stability Strategic Strength Structure Success Support Teamwork Temperance Thankfulness Thoroughness Thoughtfulness Timeliness Tolerance Traditionalism Trustworthiness Truth-seeking Understanding Uniqueness Unity Usefulness Vision Vitality

List of values was taken from www.mindtools.com

In the adjacent list, circle your most important values and write them on this page

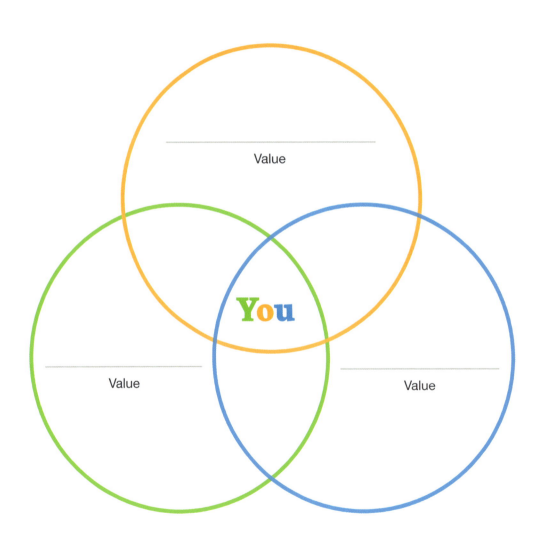

Accountability Accuracy Achievement Adventurous Altruism Ambition

Assertiveness Balance Being the best Belonging Boldness Calmness

Carefulness Challenge Cheerfulness Clear-mindedness Commitment

Community Compassion Competitiveness Consistency Contentment

Continuity Contribution Control Cooperation Correctness Courtesy

Creativity Curiosity Decisiveness Democratic Dependability Determination

Devoutness Diligence Discipline Discretion Diversity Dynamism

Economy Effectiveness Efficiency Elegance Empathy Enjoyment

Enthusiasm Equality Excellence Excitement Expertise Exploration

Expressiveness Fairness Faith Family Fidelity Fitness Fluency Focus

Freedom Fun Generosity Goodness Grace Growth Happiness

Hard work Health Helping society Holiness Honesty Honor Humility

Improvement Independence Ingenuity Inner harmony Inquisitiveness

Insightfulness Intelligence Intellectual status Intuition Joy Justice

Kindness Leadership Legacy Love Loyalty Making a difference Mastery

Merit Obedience Openness Order Originality Patriotism Perfection

Piety Positivity Practicality Preparedness Professionalism Prudence

Quality Reliability Resourcefulness Restraint Results-oriented Rigor

Security Self-actualization Self-control Selflessness Self-reliance

Sensitivity Serenity Service Shrewdness Simplicity Soundness Speed

Spontaneity Stability Strategic Strength Structure Success Support

Teamwork Temperance Thankfulness Thoroughness Thoughtfulness

Timeliness Tolerance Traditionalism Trustworthiness Truth-seeking

Understanding Uniqueness Unity Usefulness Vision Vitality

List of values was taken from www.mindtools.com

The sailboat illustrates a space to explore: write, doodle, brainstorm, etc.

Reflections

How was the Values Discovery exercise for you?

	LOW	MEDIUM	HIGH
Confusing	○	○	○
Curiosity	○	○	○
Exciting	○	○	○

> It's not hard to make decisions once you know what your values are. *- Roy E. Disney*

03.

Surfacing Assumptions

BENEFIT:

Assumptions are your current map of the world. By examining them, you can begin to explore uncharted waters.

01. Warm-up to Your Futures
02. Values Discovery
03. Surfacing Assumptions
04. Other Futures
05. Backcasting
06. Implications
07. Reflection

If your current trajectory continues, what will your life be like in five years? How about ten?

Inspired by Peter Bishop and Andy Hines and their book "Thinking About the Future."

Most of us have thought about what our future selves might be doing. Whether we're happy with where we are or ready to disrupt ourselves, we think about the future. Know it or not, we tend to have a view of what our future might hold. Typically, these thoughts reflect our core values, which were articulated in the previous section. It will be important to keep our core values in mind throughout the rest of the exercises, as they are an articulation of our core selves.

Even if we know our core values, usually our expected future is unspoken and unacknowledged. It often appears in our minds as a continuation of what's currently happening. In this section we will uncover what you expect your future to be like. These expectations are also called assumptions.

Assumptions are beliefs we have about the future. They are not bad – they are often made unconsciously and so it is important to surface them in order to know what your beliefs about the future are. This exercise will help unearth your assumptions about your expected future. The expected future you create will be the foundation for your exploration of other futures in the exercises to follow.

If things continue as they are, my life in five years will look like...

I will be _____ years old.

I will be living in _____.

My main activities will be _____.

The greatest changes in my life are _____

_____.

EVIDENCE

What must **stay the same** for the above to be true?

[   ]

EVIDENCE

What must **change** for the above to be true?

[   ]

These are your assumptions

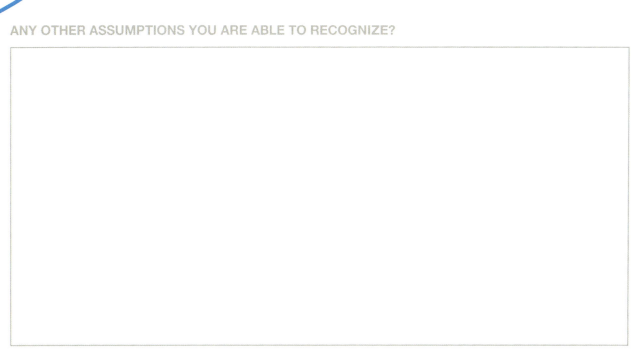

ANY OTHER ASSUMPTIONS YOU ARE ABLE TO RECOGNIZE?

Further exploring your assumptions

I AM WORRIED THAT THE FOLLOWING MIGHT HAPPEN IN THE FUTURE:

I WANT THE FOLLOWING TO HAPPEN IN THE FUTURE:

I EXPECT THE FOLLOWING TO HAPPEN IN THE FUTURE:

Inspired by Peter Bishop's Teach The Future - teachthefuture.org.

Let's try an expanded version

Utilizing any method you like - drawing, writing, storyboarding, or even creating a "day in the life" - expand upon your expected future. Go deeper. What might your life look like in five years, if current conditions continue as they are today? Start anywhere and use the whole space!

This is your expected future!

How does your expected future align with your core values? Are there other values you'd like to add after further reflection?

Reflections

How was the Surfacing Assumptions exercise for you?

	LOW	MEDIUM	HIGH
Confusing	○	○	○
Curiosity	○	○	○
Exciting	○	○	○

Your assumptions are your windows on the world. Scrub them off every once in a while, or the light won't come in. - *Alan Alda*

04.

Other Futures

BENEFIT

By pushing your thinking to the edges of possibility, new horizons will begin to appear.

01. Warm-up to Your Futures
02. Values Discovery
03. Surfacing Assumptions
04. Other Futures
05. Backcasting
06. Implications
07. Reflection

Futures I've never considered before!

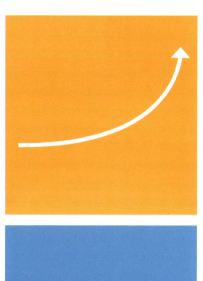

Now that you know your expected future, break it! The fun part about working with futures is that there are a number of different futures possible - not just one. The Alternative Futures method is one tool you can use to uncover what your different futures might look like.

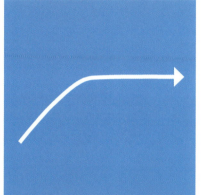

Alternative Futures has been best described by futurist Wendy Schultz as "maximizing difference." Meaning, you are stretching yourself away from your expected future in order to explore extremely different futures, You may find useful nuggets of inspiration and innovation within your Alternative Futures.

This exercise is meant to challenge what you know to be true today, as well as challenge your assumptions about tomorrow. Through this exercise, we'll introduce you to a few ideas that will help stretch your thinking. Refrain from thinking about these futures as positive or negative. Rather, think about them as interesting studies into what might be within the realm of possibility.

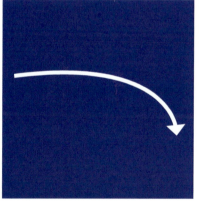

How does this change the way you view your present? Let your imagination go!

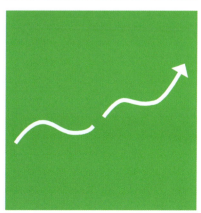

Jim Dator at the University of Hawaii published "Alternative Futures at the Manoa School." The alternative futures descriptions in this section and the illustrations were inspired by Stuart Candy.

Alternative Futures

Alternative Futures is a generative way to explore extreme futures within the realm of possibility. Essentially, this is another view of the cone of possibilities you were introduced to in the previous chapter. You can think of the realm of possibilities, indicated on the opposite page, as a sectional slice of the cone of possibilities. This displays futures that are both possible and plausible, but vastly different from one another. Each of the four Alternative Futures below - growth, collapse, constraint, and transformation - are archetypical futures that you can use as prompts for creative exploration. While far from absolute, each of these futures allows you to stretch your thinking beyond the current status-quo into realms you may not have considered before. This is a helpful exercise in breaking from the norm and can help spur futures concepts that may not have been uncovered if thinking only about utopian outcomes of current states.

Typically, and especially in the United States, people tend to make their expected futures (from the previous exercise) closest to a growth archetype. This means that during the Alternative Futures exercise you will be challenged to think beyond what you may hope for yourself and instead test yourself by truly being exploratory with all the archetypes in this exercise.

Not all cultures naturally relate to a growth scenario. It is interesting to consider what future you most associate with, what externalities (both internal and external), as well as recent events, could cause you to be drawn to one archetype over another. An honest assessment of where you initially gravitate toward will help you later identify which future possibility speaks to you as your preferred future scenario.

Illustrations inspired by Stuart Candy.

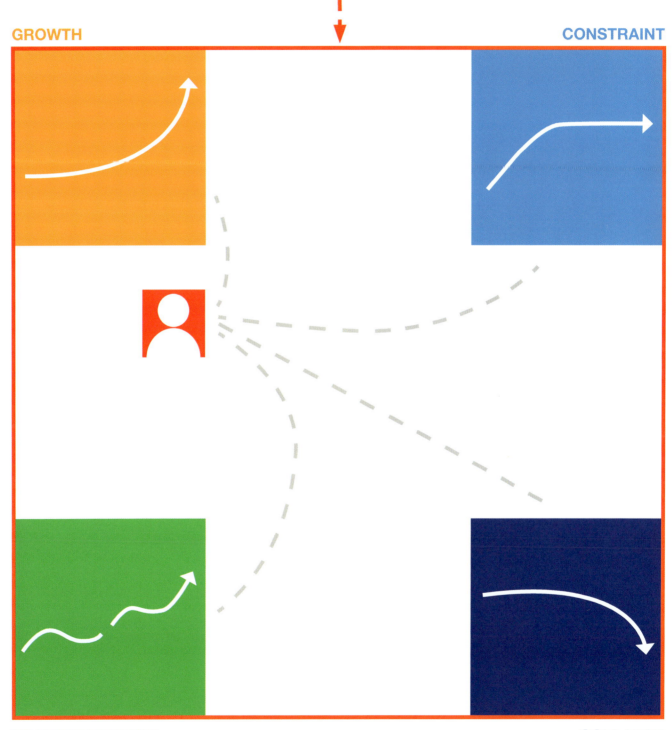

Growth Scenario

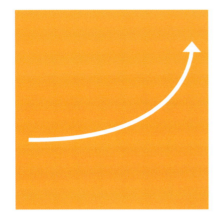

The Growth Scenario is a future where most elements of life continue to increase. For example, education, population, income disparity, technological advances, and potentially many more. This is different than your expected future as the growth of society may have unintended consequences you haven't considered before. A Growth future looks at a possibility when life as you know it is exaggerated.

STEP 1
In my career, my personal life, or socially, I spend the majority of my time doing:

TODAY

STEP 2
20 YEARS IN THE FUTURE

The year is 20_____. I am _____ years old. If I continue to _____
                                          (age)   (action from above circle)

_____ I will be better at _____ but
                                                                                  (verb)

worse at _____.
                                       (verb)

This makes me _____
                                         (feeling)

because _____.

STEP 3

Now that you have filled out one Growth future possibility, answer the questions below. What part of this future resonates with you? Which part makes you feel concerned or uncertain?

CINDY

Currently, I spend the majority of my time caring for my grandson.

The year is 2036, and I am 85 years old. If I continue to care for my grandson, I will be better at providing care for my family, and I will be enriched from my experiences with him but maybe worse at enjoying life for myself. This makes me feel cautious about the next 20 years because I want to be able to explore new hobbies and activities, find balance, and enjoy my retirement.

WHAT I LIKE ABOUT MY GROWTH FUTURE:

FEARS AND CONCERNS I HAVE ABOUT MY GROWTH FUTURE:

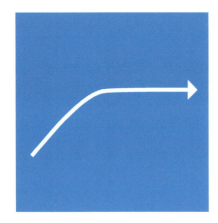

Constraint Scenario

The Constraint Scenario is a type of future in which elements of life are deliberately managed - either by a person or group (government, corporation, organization, etc.) - sometimes to maintain a societal balance. The exercise below will help give you a glimpse into one potential Constraint future.

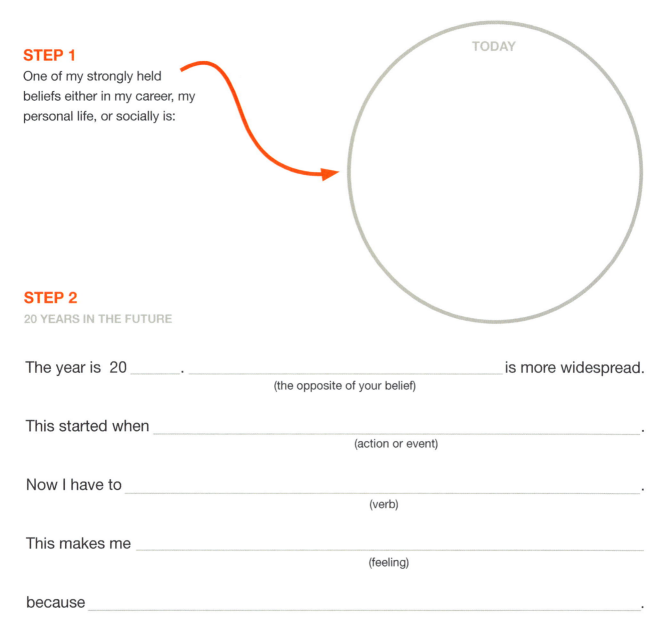

STEP 1
One of my strongly held beliefs either in my career, my personal life, or socially is:

STEP 2
20 YEARS IN THE FUTURE

The year is 20 _____. _____ is more widespread.
(the opposite of your belief)

This started when _____.
(action or event)

Now I have to _____.
(verb)

This makes me _____
(feeling)

because _____.

STEP 3

Now that you have filled out one Constraint future possibility, answer the questions below. What part of this future resonates with you? Which part makes you feel concerned or uncertain?

WHAT I LIKE ABOUT MY CONSTRAINT FUTURE:

FEARS AND CONCERNS I HAVE ABOUT MY CONSTRAINT FUTURE:

HARPER

Currently, one of my strongly held social beliefs is that the cost of living should reflect income, not location.

The year is 2036; cost of living is more inflated than ever. This started when minimum wage was kept at a constant instead of increasing proportionally to cost of living. Now I have to work two jobs to sustain my lifestyle. This makes me feel frustrated and angry because I want to feel value for my profession and my passion, not just make ends meet, or even worse, barely survive.

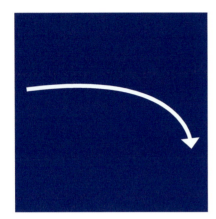

Collapse Scenario

The Collapse Scenario is a future in which your familiar life is disintegrating. This breakdown is causing implications across many sectors including personal, societal, economic, governmental, and spiritual.

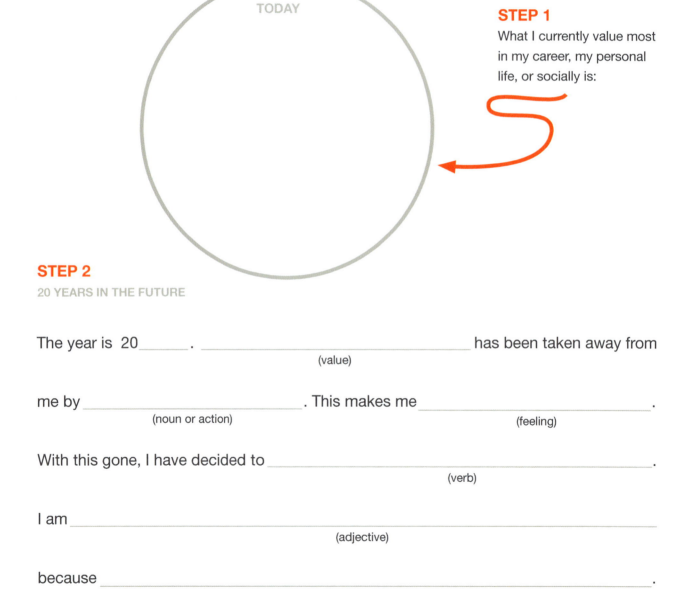

STEP 1
What I currently value most in my career, my personal life, or socially is:

STEP 2
20 YEARS IN THE FUTURE

The year is 20_____ . _____ has been taken away from
                              (value)

me by _____ . This makes me _____ .
         (noun or action)   (feeling)

With this gone, I have decided to _____ .
                                                  (verb)

I am _____
                    (adjective)

because _____ .

STEP 3

Now that you have filled out one Collapse future possibility, answer the questions below. What part of this future resonates with you? Which part makes you feel concerned or uncertain?

CINDY

Currently, I place the most value in my family.

The year is 2036. My family has been taken away from me by distance. This makes me a little frightful.

With them gone, I have decided to engage in community activities and volunteering. I am anxious about the next few years because it means I will have to grow a new social group on my own for the first time since I was married.

WHAT I LIKE ABOUT MY COLLAPSE FUTURE:

FEARS AND CONCERNS I HAVE ABOUT MY COLLAPSE FUTURE:

Transformation Scenario

In this future scenario, remarkable change has happened. This change has transformed the way we think. One past example might be the sudden adoption of smartphones. For many, imagining life without the technology we carry in our pockets is difficult. Transformation futures welcome a new normal - societal, spiritual or technological.

STEP 1

TODAY

In my career, my personal life, or socially,

_____
(keeps me up at night)

It keeps me up at night because

_____.

STEP 2

20 YEARS IN THE FUTURE

The year is 20_____. _____ is no longer my
　　　　　　　　　　　　(the thing that keeps me up at night)

concern, due to _____.
　　　　　　　　　　　　　　(action or event)

Now I am able to focus on _____.
　　　　　　　　　　　　　　　　(verb)

I am _____
　　　　　(feeling)

because _____.

STEP 3

Now that you have filled out one Transformation future possibility, answer the questions below. What part of this future resonates with you? Which part makes you feel concerned or uncertain?

HARPER

Currently, professional growth keeps me up at night. I'm worried that I'm too old to begin a new career in design.

The year is 2036, and professional growth is no longer my concern, due to my enrollment in graduate design classes. Now I am able to focus on my future as an art and design professor. I am excited and driven toward the next several years because I can take the steps toward being self sufficient and successful while fostering passion for my craft.

WHAT I LIKE ABOUT MY TRANSFORMATION FUTURE:

FEARS AND CONCERNS I HAVE ABOUT MY TRANSFORMATION FUTURE:

GROWTH

Freestyle

Utilizing any method you like - drawing, writing, storyboarding or even creating a "day in the life" - expand upon your Alternative Futures from the pages prior to get a bit more in-depth. The Mad Libs you explored were one way to approach creating other futures - how else might you explore each future scenario? While working through this exercise, think particularly about how your core values play a role in each of these scenarios. How can you continue to achieve or live by your core values within these worlds?

TRANSFORMATION

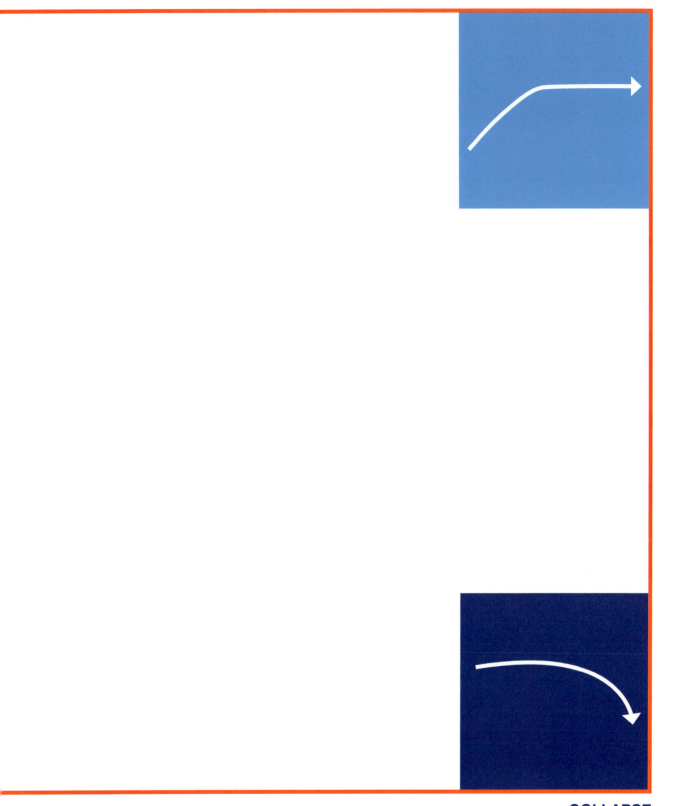

Bonus points!
Test drive your futures

Earlier in this book we introduced the idea that foresight is a collaborative discipline. Personal futures explorations are no exception. Outside eyes, or someone to bounce ideas off of, is unbelievably valuable. Not only can they help you assess the plausibility of your future scenarios, but they can also help you poke holes in your assessment, or consider outcomes you haven't thought of yet. When thinking about your futures, sometimes those who know you best can shed light on the plausibility and actionability of the futures you have created.

After completing your Alternative Futures (i.e. right now!) is a great time to get another pair of eyes on them. Remember that the Alternative Futures method is meant to help you envision extreme futures, some of which may stretch the realm of plausibility. That's okay! External feedback on this creative exercise is still highly valuable, if only to start a conversation about future possibilities. For feedback like this, try asking an immediate family member, spouse, or close friend. In other words, someone who knows you well, and has a good sense of your unique capabilities, accomplishments, and goals. The Mad Libs you just created tend to be quite full of emotion, so make sure you ask someone you feel comfortable speaking honestly about these emotions with.

Asking for guidance and feedback will help you assess how you have completed these exercises so far. Test driving your futures with others also will add an element of accountability. Through the discussion, you may just recognize one of these futures as your preferable future scenario. Talking through this recognition with someone else will help you think of your identified future as more tangible, which is the first step toward making it a reality.

This is a great space to record feedback you received and how that made you think about your Alternative Futures!

Reflections

How was the Other Futures exercise for you?

	LOW	MEDIUM	HIGH
Confusing	○	○	○
Curiosity	○	○	○
Exciting	○	○	○

> Any useful statement about the future should at first appear to be ridiculous. *- Jim Dator*

05.

Backcasting

BENEFIT

Plotting the course to your desired, plausible future.

01. Warm-up to Your Futures
02. Values Discovery
03. Surfacing Assumptions
04. Other Futures
05. Backcasting
06. Implications
07. Reflection

Making the seemingly intangible, tangible.

We hope you're enjoying exploring futures as much as we do! The next goal is to apply those futures to your life right now. One of the strengths of looking at future possibilities is that they will help you better make decisions in your present.

The first step in backcasting is outlining a preferred future for yourself so that we can work back from that future to the present. The goal of backcasting is to articulate what actions you need to take now, to start making your way toward your preferred future. What is so interesting is that there are often many small changes you can identify today in order to start on your path toward your preferred future. It's simpler than you might imagine.

Given all the exercises we have done so far, this will allow you space to think about what it is you truly want for yourself. Take a moment now to look back over the futures you have created for yourself, and craft one that you can use as your "preferred" future for this exercise (space provided on p. 69). Your preferred future may not be one of the archetypes you have already explored, in fact, it is rarely one of the extremes. It may lie somewhere else in the cone of possibilities, and will probably be a combination of futures you want to attain and those you want to avoid. We encourage you to use a preferred future which feels right to you - either an "other future" you have already created, or a new combination of them. While the Alternative Futures explored extremes, your preferred future should take into account plausibility - it should be a future you can see yourself actively working on and making progress toward.

As with any futures exercise, try not to manage it - just let your ideas flow. You can do this backcasting exercise many times! It is meant to serve as a guide, and should be revisited every six months to a year.

> How do you get to a preferred future? Change the story you tell yourself about the future you want to live in.
> - *Brian David Johnson*

Backcasting.
A roadmap guiding you
to where you want to go.

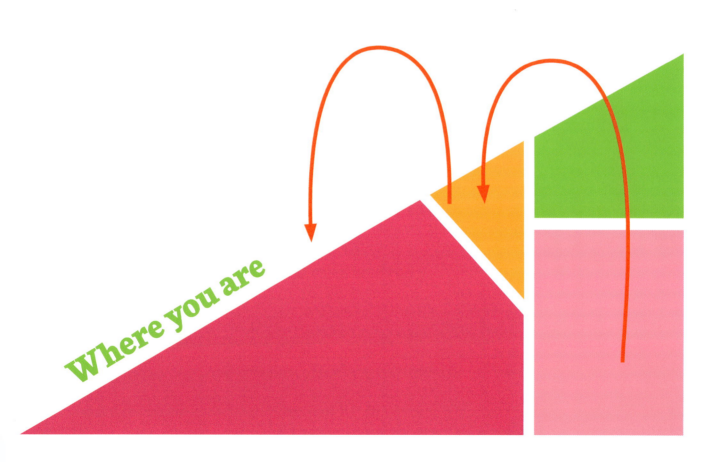

Where you are

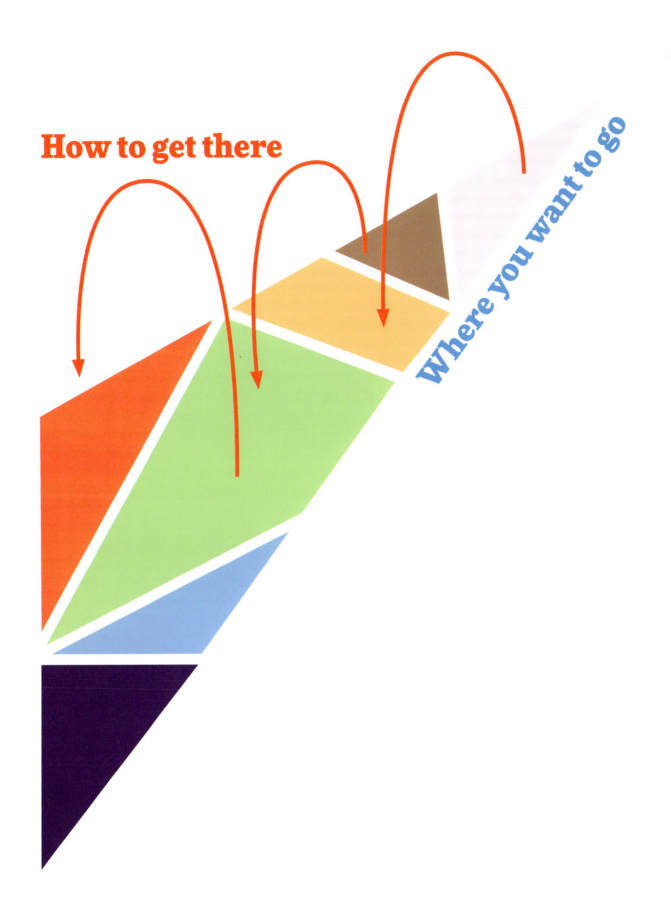

Backcasting worksheet

After reflecting on your four Alternative Futures, take some time in the space to the right to craft your preferred future. The previous example of a preferred future was taking time to travel and explore the world for a few years. This may be a future you align with and emerged from your Alternative Futures, or it could be something completely different! The key is to try to be as specific as possible (even though we know the future is a hazy business).

Once you have articulated your preferred future, you will work backwards to create actionable steps to get closer to realizing that future.

Step 5 ←

Today

I am _____ years old.

My parents are _____ years old.

My children/grandchildren are this old
_____

To achieve my five-year goal (step 4), starting today I need to:
_____
_____
_____
_____

Step 4 ←

Five Years From Today

I am _____ years old.

My parents are _____ years old.

My children/grandchildren are this old
_____

To achieve my 10-year goal (step 3), at year five I need to:
_____
_____
_____
_____

BEGIN HERE **Step 1** Write your preferred future in this space.

Step 2

Start your backcasting in this column and move to the left across the pages filling out one section at a time.

Step 3

Ten years from today

I am _____ years old.

My parents are _____ years old.

My children/grandchildren are this old _____

To achieve my 15-year goal (step 2), at year 10 I need to:

Fifteen years from today

I am _____ years old.

My parents are _____ years old.

My children/grandchildren are this old _____

To achieve my preferred future, at year 15 I need to:

What is the biggest change you need to make to get to your preferred future?

Reflections

How was the Backcasting exercise for you?

	LOW	MEDIUM	HIGH
Confusing	○	○	○
Curiosity	○	○	○
Exciting	○	○	○

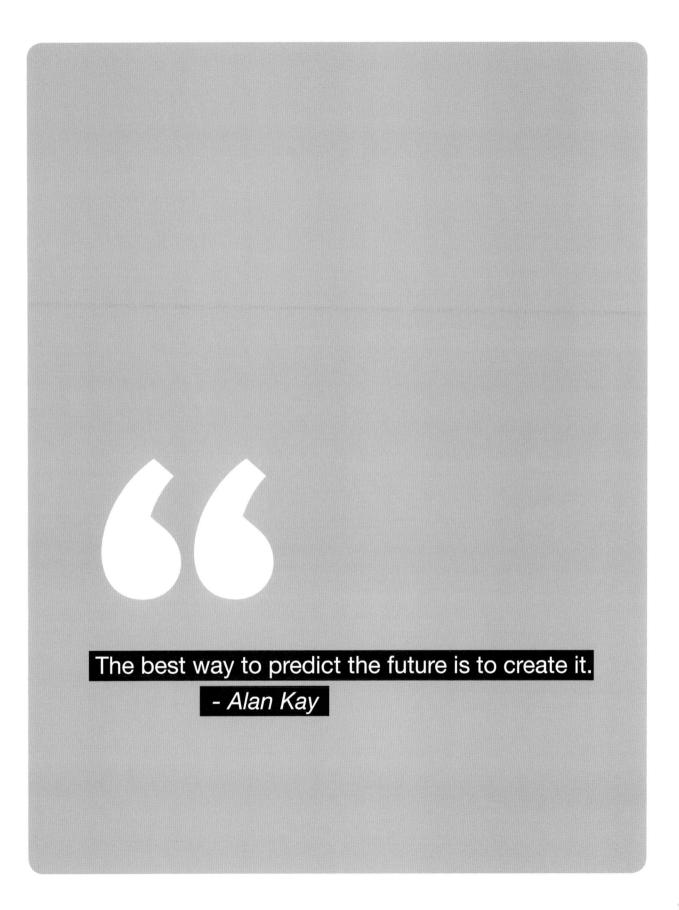

06.
Implications

BENEFIT

Every decision has a ripple effect. You need to understand the wake created to choose the best direction.

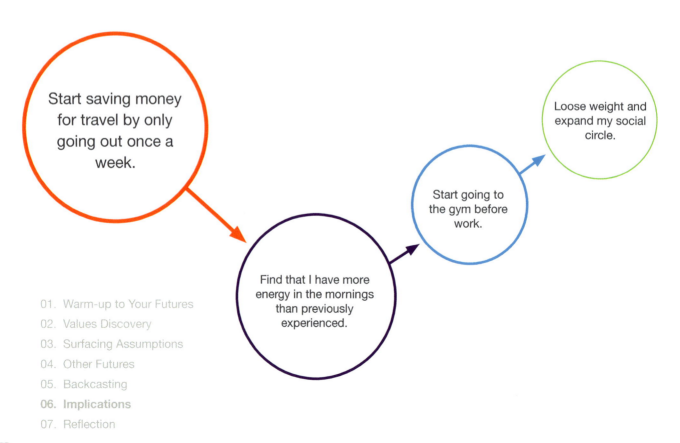

01. Warm-up to Your Futures
02. Values Discovery
03. Surfacing Assumptions
04. Other Futures
05. Backcasting
06. **Implications**
07. Reflection

Take one step, then take a couple more!

You've come a long way! From vague thoughts about your future to identifying your values, exploring multiple extreme potential futures, through creating a stepped plan on how to get to your preferred one. You may be asking yourself, how will the actions I take toward my preferred future impact other aspects of my life? Great question.

Your next exercise will be a tool called the Futures Wheel. The Futures Wheel is used to explore the impacts and consequences of a decision or action. For this exercise, focus on the preferred future you created for the Backcasting exercise. (There are additional copies of the Futures Wheel in the back of the book, so you can do this exercise many times with many different futures!) Start with a specific action or decision in the center of the Futures Wheel. Specificity is important here, as a vague start will yield vague results, and your goal is to be as clear as possible. In the Futures Wheel on p. 74, you will see many different circles branching off - this is to allow you space to explore several implication arms. The diagram on the adjacent page is an example of one implication arm.

Once you have a starting point, ask yourself: What is likely to happen first if this decision or action moves forward? What might be some immediate consequences? Write your thoughts in the circle titled "implications." Next, select one of those implications or consequences and ask yourself again, what is likely to happen as a result of this? Consequences? Repeat this exploration until you have reached third or even fourth round implications. Remember to challenge your own assumptions as you go through - sometimes just questioning your own reasoning opens up doors you never noticed before. There are no right or wrong answers – let's get going!

The Futures Wheel was created by Jerome C. Glenn in 1971.

CHANGE AND IMPLICATION

Another way to look at implications is as if they are cause and effect. This method doesn't map one-to-one, however, is helpful as an example of a string of implications.

Change
David slings stone at Goliath and hits him in the forehead.

Implication
Goliath falls and is killed.

Change
Goliath falls and is killed.

Implication
Philistine army sees Goliath's death, panics and runs.

Change
Philistine army sees Goliath's death, panics and runs.

Implication
Israel's army sees Philistines break and run, Jews pursue and rout Philistine army, killing many and taking spoils.

Michael G. Miller, "Thinking About Second & Third Order Effects: A Sample (And Simple) Methodology"

Futures Wheel

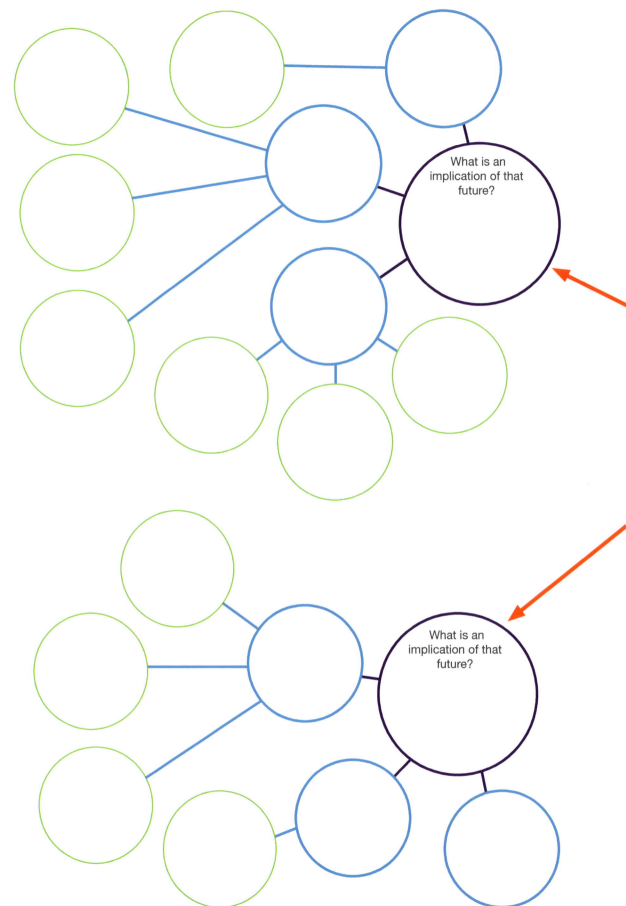

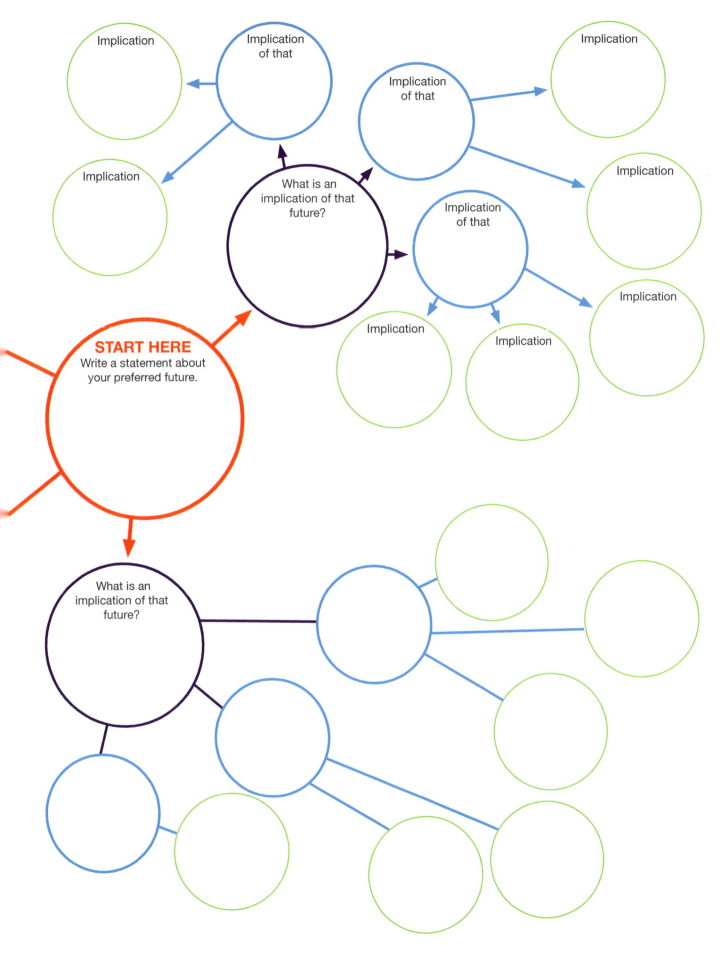

Was there an implication you didn't expect? How does that affect the way you think about your preferred future?

Reflections

How was the Implications exercise for you?

	LOW	MEDIUM	HIGH
Confusing	○	○	○
Curiosity	○	○	○
Exciting	○	○	○

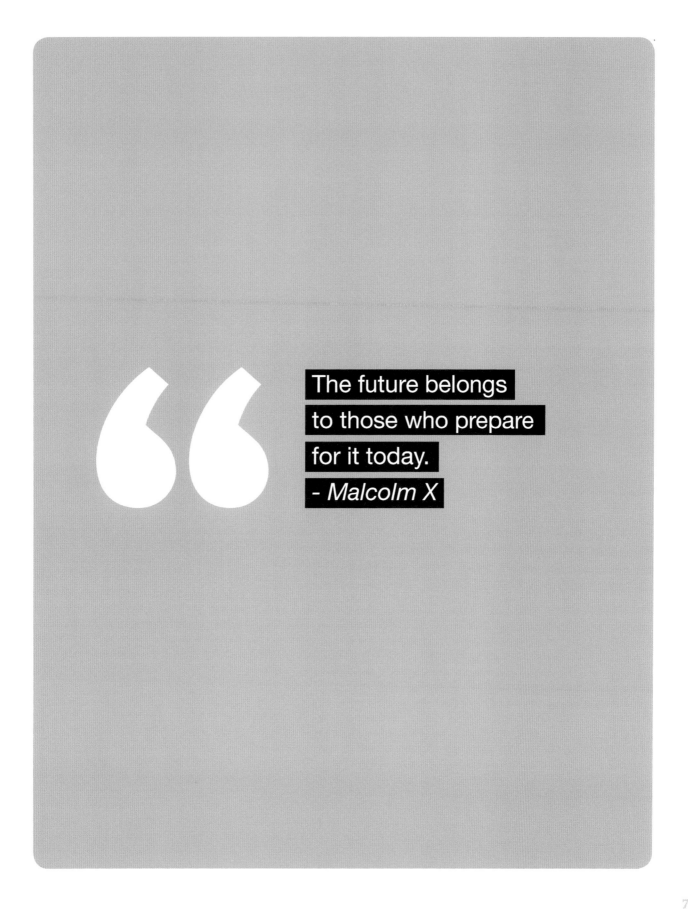

07.

Reflection

BENEFIT

Mapping your journey allows you to retrace where you've been in order to understand where you can go.

You did it! You workshopped your future!

Before moving on, take a moment to reflect on how the exercises included in each section changed your thought process. Glance back at the reflection sections after each exercise, and copy your responses on the adjacent page. What patterns do you see? Did you respond better to some exercises than others? Are several worth a revisit? You have covered a lot of ground; take a moment to reflect on whether you are thinking differently about your futures and how your thoughts have changed.

01. Warm-up to Your Futures
02. Values Discovery
03. Surfacing Assumptions
04. Other Futures
05. Backcasting
06. Implications
07. Reflection

		LOW	MEDIUM	HIGH
Values Discovery	Confusing	○	○	○
	Curiosity	○	○	○
	Exciting	○	○	○
Surfacing Assumptions	Confusing	○	○	○
	Curiosity	○	○	○
	Exciting	○	○	○
Other Futures	Confusing	○	○	○
	Curiosity	○	○	○
	Exciting	○	○	○
Backcasting	Confusing	○	○	○
	Curiosity	○	○	○
	Exciting	○	○	○
Implications	Confusing	○	○	○
	Curiosity	○	○	○
	Exciting	○	○	○

Notice a change?

Utilizing any method you like - drawing, writing, storyboarding, or any other - capture how your thoughts have changed, and what it is you would like to focus on moving forward. Start anywhere you like; this is your space to expose discoveries!

CHAPTER FIVE

What to do next

ABOUT THIS CHAPTER

A summation of what you have accomplished will help propel you forward.

Quick Recap

You just went through seven exercises to help make your futures more tangible. You've learned that there is no such thing as one definite future. Instead, there is a range of possible futures to explore and examine. Most of all, the future is still being made! Armed with the tools in this workbook, you are now on your way to taking on a futures mindset.

So what does that mean? It means it is time orient yourself toward your futures. Use the futures you have outlined, test them and revise them continuously. Try taking the steps you outlined in the Backcasting tool - the first steps toward your preferred future. Only you can live your futures, and your time starts now! Most importantly, these exercises aren't just "one and done"; revisit your futures in six months and adjust them as your assumptions and life circumstances change. The future is a work in progress. Use additional tear-outs in the back of this book to do these exercises again when you desire.

This set of tools was curated to help you think about your personal futures, but there are a lot more out there. Once you start exercising your foresight mind, a long view lens will become increasingly natural. Continue to use these tools, and try them on topics other than yourself.

Most of all, stay curious. The future is always changing, and new possibilities are popping up all the time. Hopefully this book has served as an introduction and overview to the world of foresight. Your quest: continue to explore it.

Foresight, for those brave enough to consider something different

Final thoughts...

Before you move on to futures of your own making, capture your most impactful moments from this experience.

BIGGEST DISCOVERY
What did you discover about your futures that left the biggest impression?

BIGGEST CONSIDERATION
What did these exercises uncover that will need more consideration?

BIGGEST DESIRE
What is it that you cannot wait to try, build or explore? What do you now feel the need to do that you haven't felt before?

VALUES
Did they change or stay the same?

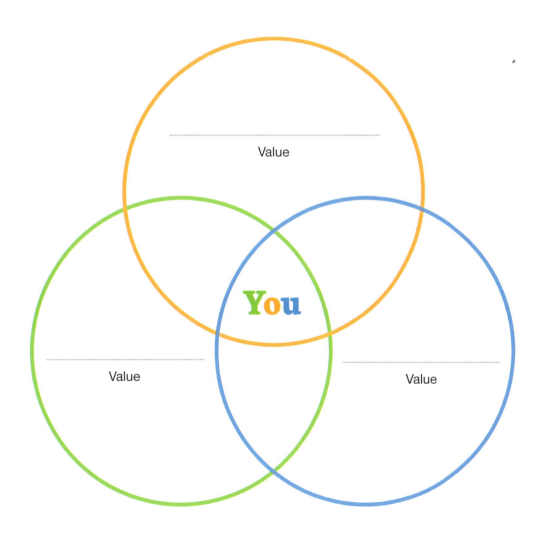

CHAPTER SIX

Back of the book stuff

ABOUT THIS CHAPTER

All of the extras - references for more reading, about the authors, and contact information.

> I've come to believe that things are getting better and better and worse and worse, faster and faster, simultaneously
> - Tom Atlee

Contact us!

Have questions or feedback? Using this book in a way you think might be totally unlike how we intended? We'd love to hear from you! Let us know how you have adopted or edited the tools in this book. We are always improving and folding in feedback. Let us know yours!

www.wtforesight.com

Alida Draudt
alida@wtforesight.com

Julia Rose West
julia@wtforesight.com

EXPLORE THESE!
The following are resources we used and referenced throughout this workbook. We have included books, a podcast, and several organizations we highly recommend.

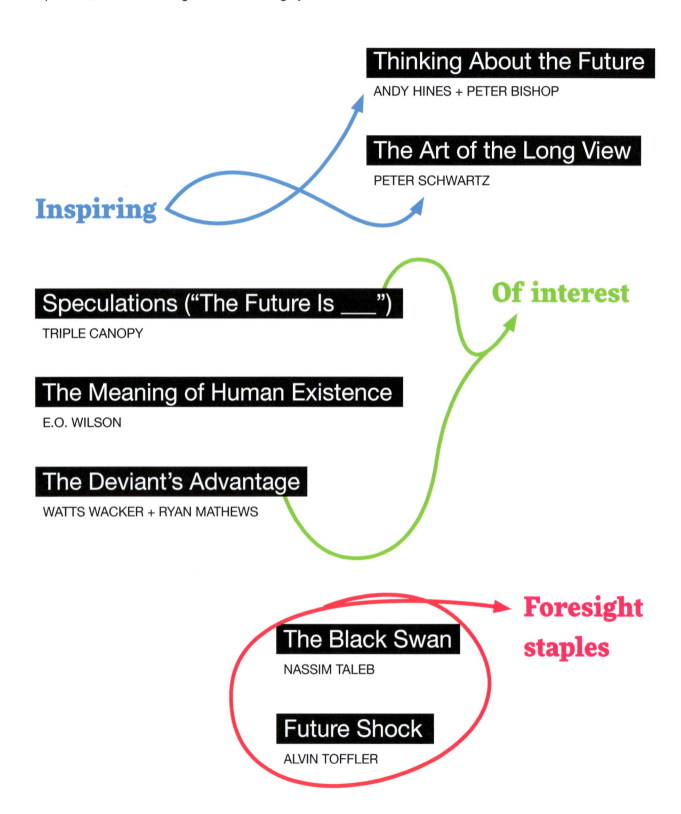

Further learning

Institute for the Future
IFTF.ORG

The Long Now Foundation
LONGNOW.ORG

Teach The Future
TEACHTHEFUTURE.ORG

Science Fiction Prototyping
BRIAN DAVID JOHNSON

Something to aspire to!

For consideration

The Trend Forecaster's Handbook
MARTIN RAYMOND

Personal Futures Workbook
VERNE WHEELWRIGHT

Listen

Flash Forward (Podcast)
ROSE EVELETH

INTERVIEWS WITH THE AUTHORS

We asked you to go through several incredibly introspective exercises, and thought it was only fair we share some personal insights with you as well.

Alida

How have you recognized the gap between expected and preferred futures for yourself?

I have always had a desire to understand an array of possibilities, even for mundane tasks. As a child, I could barely decide on one outfit each morning as every day held multiple possibilities. Instead, I chose outfits that would account for every possibility! As an adult, I continually build future personal scenarios. Whether it is about heading to the grocery store, or larger career moves, I run scenarios of potential outcomes. I admit, not all these scenarios are shared out loud, but it is a constant activity for me. I think the acceptance of inevitable change has helped me embrace the gap between my current expected and potential futures. It has helped me balance the immediate and the long term - knowing they are always in flux.

What frightens you most about one of your futures?

Social equality is incredibly important to me. When working through my Constraint future, I had to confront the idea that we might never reach social equality in the United States, or that we may even revert back to a society which is even less accepting than today. This is a fear and struggle not only for me but for millions of American citizens. While it is something I am actively working against, I find it useful to revisit this potential world - if only to keep my focus on forward progression.

What is your favorite foresight tool?

One of my favorite parts of foresight work is creating design fictions from futures scenarios, particularly writing dystopian or collapse futures. I love to imagine the innovation possibility in less-than-ideal worlds. Imagining worlds very different from our own allows me to explore far-reaching corners of my creativity while simultaneously remaining grounded in the nature of human reality - in the psychology of humanness. This tension between far out and grounded has a unique way of holding my intrigue.

James Dator said that any useful statement about the future should at first appear to be ridiculous. What is a ridiculous statement you have about the future?

One of our plausible futures is that humans will begin to date and fall in love with robots. The line between human and machine will continue to blur until there may be no distinction but instead a spectrum of humanness. We have already begun. Joint replacements and pace makers are commonplace. Samsung has secured a patent to create virtual reality enabled contact lenses. The transhumanist movement is growing in popularity. Soon we will all have pieces of machines in us. At that point, how do we define human versus machine? At what percentage? It will be a difficult line to draw in the sand, and I think before the turn of the century we will find ourselves accepting a wider definition of what humans are.

Julia

How did you get into foresight?

On my mother's side, the majority of people are scientists. I started out in college as a physics major. My time as a physics major did not last long. I was taking a photography class as an elective and loved it. I told my dad I was going to switch to photography. He asked me to consider other creative options and their probability for success. Photography is a highly competitive field. He was basically saying, *"Great, you want to do something creative, go for it, but research it and consider other possible futures."* After evaluation and research, I eventually settled on graphic design. I worked for years as a visual designer, creative director, UX and UI designer. At one point in my career, I was part of an executive team. I was involved in making decisions that affected the entire organization. I was drawn to the idea that business problems could be better solved by applying similar design methodologies. I started researching business schools. In addition, my husband, Aaron, and I would often discuss foresight and how the coolest career in the world is a futurist. At one point Aaron said, *"How do you get that job?"* When I heard that California College of the Arts was offering a Strategic Foresight MBA, I applied. It was the perfect combination of my past (design), my then present (business), and my future (foresight). At the time, I did not fully understand what foresight was or what a futurist did, but I was fortunate I had enough foresight to take the risk and enough grit to succeed. The irony is that the discipline of foresight is very scientific in its approach, so I have come full circle.

What is your preferred future?

My preferred future is one where everyone has access to his or her futures. I think we should be introducing foresight or at least the concept of it to children. Peter Bishop is doing amazing things introducing foresight into curriculums with his organization *Teach the Future*. It is important for children to know that they have choices and a variety of futures to strive for, not just one set goal or planned path. I think currently foresight is for a few, for the privileged. Sometimes we are forced to think about other futures out of desperation – refugees fleeing Syria, for example. Other times, we must have all of our basic needs taken care of before we can begin to take the long view. I often wonder what the differences are between someone who leaves their country, their family, and everything they are familiar with and makes the risky journey into our country in order to work a labor-intensive job picking produce versus a single mother just trying to figure out how to put dinner on the table for her family. It may appear that the immigrant is thinking far out into the future risking their life for that of their descendants. Yet the single mother is just trying to make ends meet and is living day-to-day. How can that single mother, as well as her children, have access to all their possible futures? This is a long way of saying my preferred future is for everyone to have access to their futures.

What is a ridiculous statement you have about the future?

My statement is not my own but rather Muhammad Yunus's. I know that through innovation, design, and strategy we can fundamentally change the world and solve poverty. Yunus wrote it in *Building Social Business,* "We can create a world in which the only place you would be able to see poverty is in poverty museums. Someday, school children will be taken to visit these poverty museums. They will be horrified to see the misery and indignity that innumerable people had to go through for no fault of their own. They will blame their ancestors for tolerating this inhuman condition for so long – and rightly so."

A thank you

To those I adore: I owe my inspiration, wonder and balance.

With love, Alida

My past and present – not the same without you

My Father [Scott] who always believes in his daughters – for believing in the possible future that I could be a rocket scientist and after I quickly pivoted from that future, for believing I would be successful no matter what... especially as a designer. **My Mom [Patience Joy]** for your support a thousand times over. From day one you provided me with all that you could and even more that you couldn't. Now I am 13,492 days old and your endless generosity carries on - editing, honest feedback, long phone calls, advice. Thank you. For getting me interested in horses, which launched a future of competitive barrel racing, which I never dreamed of as probable. **My love [Aaron]** you never stop challenging me and pushing me, not only to reach the possible, but to discover all my preferred futures. For embracing all my wild ideas - waffle trucks, homeless communes, MBA's, and other ventures where I want to transform the world. The future I fear most is any future that you are not part of. All my love. **Family,** the entire Weber clan and all the Weber's before me. We are scientific proof that craziness and passion are genetic. My sisters who keep me grounded and with whom I have had the fondest memories. I love you so! For my Grammy and Granddaddy, who taught me about unbearable excitement and anticipation, who always gave us girls futures to look forward to. Every moment with them was like Christmas Eve. **CCA Loves.** Going to b-school was just one future, but all the possible futures that came out of it and are still to come, were and will continue to be life changing. A nudist colony attempt, an enactment of a political system on Mars, suspicious and illegal firewood gathering, the truffle guy, Thee Parkside, all these experiences were instrumental in helping to shape who I am today and who I can be tomorrow. Finally Ali for embracing all the craziness that came with this experience. I know this is just the beginning of a few preferred and transformational futures for us. **For the people we lost in the past few years** – my brilliant and generous cousin Wendy; my mother's best friend and sweet sister - our dearest Aunt Faith; and Martha Pedroza – we carry your blessings with us each day. You are all with us in spirit.

Julia Rose West

OPTIONAL

Extras

ABOUT THIS CHAPTER

Additional copies of the exercises for your continued use.

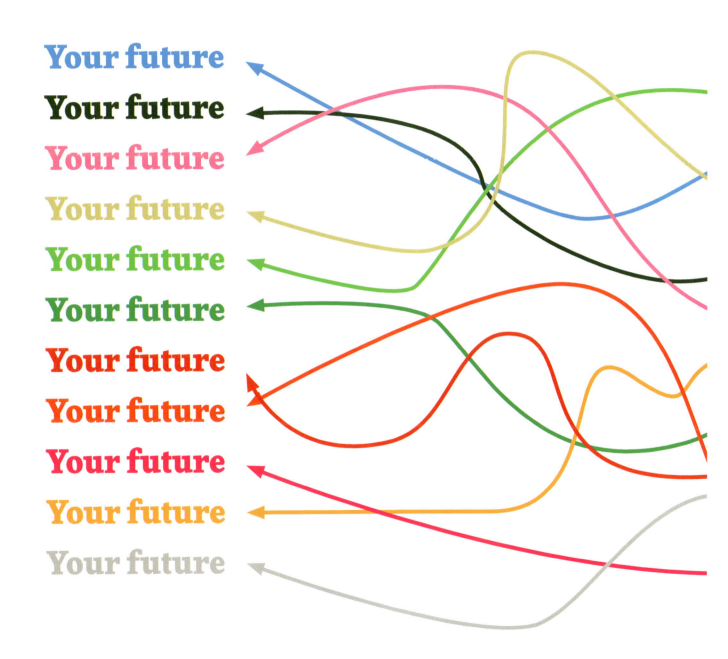

If things continue as they are, my life in five years will look like...

I will be _____ years old.

I will be living in _____.

My main activities will be _____.

The greatest changes in my life are _____

_____.

EVIDENCE

What must **stay the same** for the above to be true?

EVIDENCE

What must **change** for the above to be true?

These are your assumptions

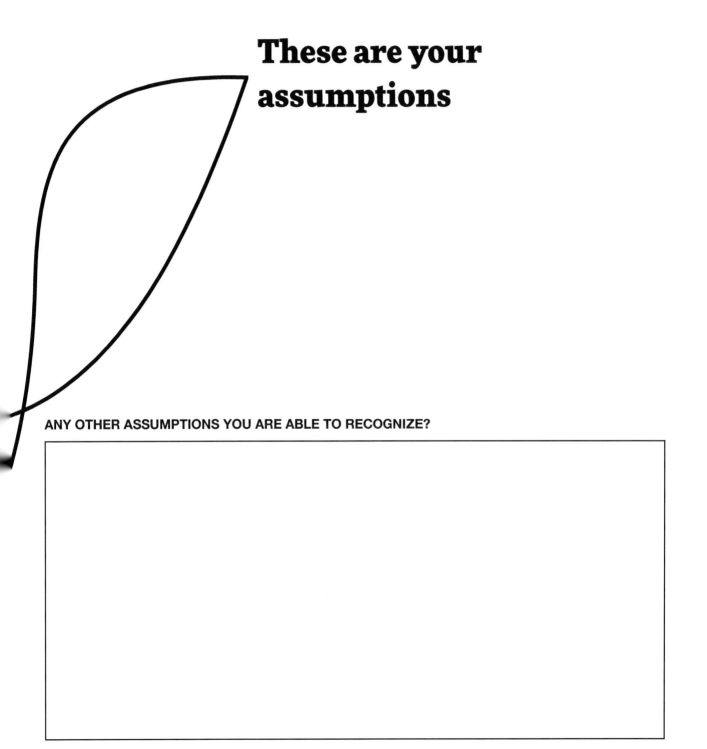

ANY OTHER ASSUMPTIONS YOU ARE ABLE TO RECOGNIZE?

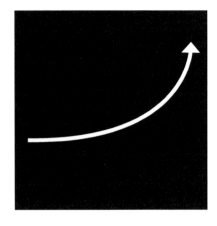

Growth Scenario

The Growth Scenario is a future where most elements of life continue to increase. For example, education, population, income disparity, technological advances, and potentially many more. This is different than your expected future as the growth of society may have unintended consequences you haven't considered before. A Growth future looks at a possibility when life as you know it is exaggerated.

STEP 1
In my career, my personal life, or socially, I spend the majority of my time doing:

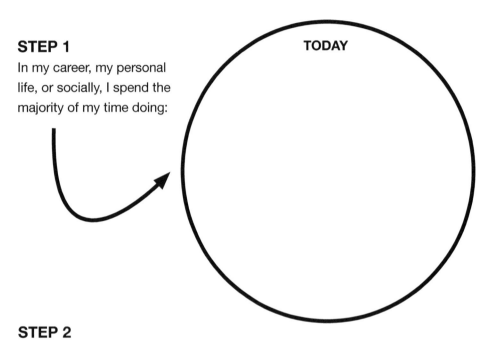

STEP 2
20 YEARS IN THE FUTURE

The year is 20_____. I am _____ years old. If I continue to _____
                              (age)   (action from above circle)

_____ I will be better at _____ but
                                                              (verb)

worse at _____.
                                                              (verb)

This makes me _____
                                                              (feeling)

because _____.

STEP 3

Now that you have filled out one Growth future possibility, answer the questions below. What part of this future resonates with you? Which part makes you feel concerned or uncertain?

WHAT I LIKE ABOUT MY GROWTH FUTURE:

FEARS AND CONCERNS I HAVE ABOUT MY GROWTH FUTURE:

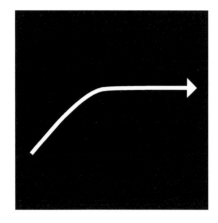

Constraint Scenario

The Constraint Scenario is a type of future in which elements of life are deliberately managed - either by a person or group (government, corporation, organization, etc.) - sometimes to maintain a societal balance. The exercise below will help give you a glimpse into one potential Constraint future.

STEP 1
One of my strongly held beliefs either in my career, my personal life, or socially is:

TODAY

STEP 2
20 YEARS IN THE FUTURE

The year is 20 _____. _____ is more widespread.
                                  (the opposite of your belief)

This started when _____.
                                  (action or event)

Now I have to _____.
                              (verb)

This makes me _____
                              (feeling)

because _____.

STEP 3
Now that you have filled out one Constraint future possibility, answer the questions below. What part of this future resonates with you? Which part makes you feel concerned or uncertain?

WHAT I LIKE ABOUT MY CONSTRAINT FUTURE:

FEARS AND CONCERNS I HAVE ABOUT MY CONSTRAINT FUTURE:

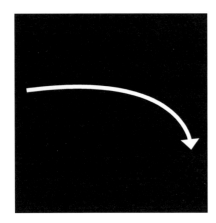

Collapse Scenario

The Collapse Scenario is a future in which your familiar life is disintegrating. This breakdown is causing implications across many sectors including personal, societal, economic, governmental, and spiritual.

TODAY

STEP 1
What I currently value most in my career, my personal life, or socially is:

STEP 2
20 YEARS IN THE FUTURE

The year is 20_____. _____ has been taken away from
                                                  (value)

me by _____. This makes me _____.
         (noun or action)   (feeling)

With this gone, I have decided to _____.
                                                          (verb)

I am _____
                          (adjective)

because _____.

STEP 3
Now that you have filled out one Collapse future possibility, answer the questions below. What part of this future resonates with you? Which part makes you feel concerned or uncertain?

WHAT I LIKE ABOUT MY COLLAPSE FUTURE:

FEARS AND CONCERNS I HAVE ABOUT MY COLLAPSE FUTURE:

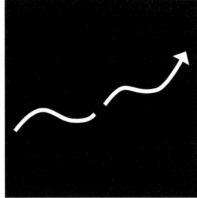

Transformation Scenario

In this future scenario, remarkable change has happened. This change has transformed the way we think. One past example might be the sudden adoption of smartphones. For many, imagining life without the technology we carry in our pockets is difficult. Transformation futures welcome a new normal - societal, spiritual or technological.

STEP 1

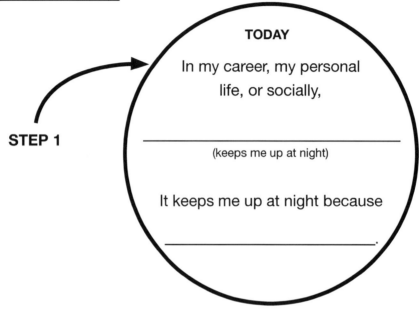

TODAY

In my career, my personal life, or socially,

_____
(keeps me up at night)

It keeps me up at night because

_____.

STEP 2
20 YEARS IN THE FUTURE

The year is 20_____. _____ is no longer my
                              (the thing that keeps me up at night)

concern, due to _____.
                                        (action or event)

Now I am able to focus on _____.
                                              (verb)

I am _____
                                        (feeling)

because _____.

STEP 3
Now that you have filled out one Transformation future possibility, answer the questions below. What part of this future resonates with you? Which part makes you feel concerned or uncertain?

WHAT I LIKE ABOUT MY TRANSFORMATION FUTURE:

FEARS AND CONCERNS I HAVE ABOUT MY TRANSFORMATION FUTURE:

Backcasting worksheet

After reflecting on your four Alternative Futures, take some time in the space to the right to craft your preferred future. The previous example of a preferred future was taking time to travel and explore the world for a few years. This may be a future you align with and emerged from your Alternative Futures, or it could be something completely different! The key is to try to be as specific as possible (even though we know the future is a hazy business).

Once you have articulated your preferred future, you will work backwards to create actionable steps to get closer to realizing that future.

Step 5 ←

Today

I am _____ years old.

My parents are _____ years old.

My children/grandchildren are this old
_____

To achieve my five-year goal (step 4), starting today I need to:
_____
_____
_____

Step 4 ←

Five Years From Today

I am _____ years old.

My parents are _____ years old.

My children/grandchildren are this old
_____

To achieve my 10-year goal (step 3), at year five I need to:
_____
_____
_____

BEGIN HERE **Step 1** Write your preferred future in this space.

Step 2

Start your backcasting in this column and move to the left across the pages filling out one section at a time.

Step 3

Ten years from today

I am _____ years old.

My parents are _____ years old.

My children/grandchildren are this old
_____

To achieve my 15-year goal (step 2), at year 10 I need to:

_____

_____

_____

Fifteen years from today

I am _____ years old.

My parents are _____ years old.

My children/grandchildren are this old
_____

To achieve my preferred future, at year 15 I need to:

_____

_____

_____

Futures Wheel

What is an implication of that future?

What is an implication of that future?

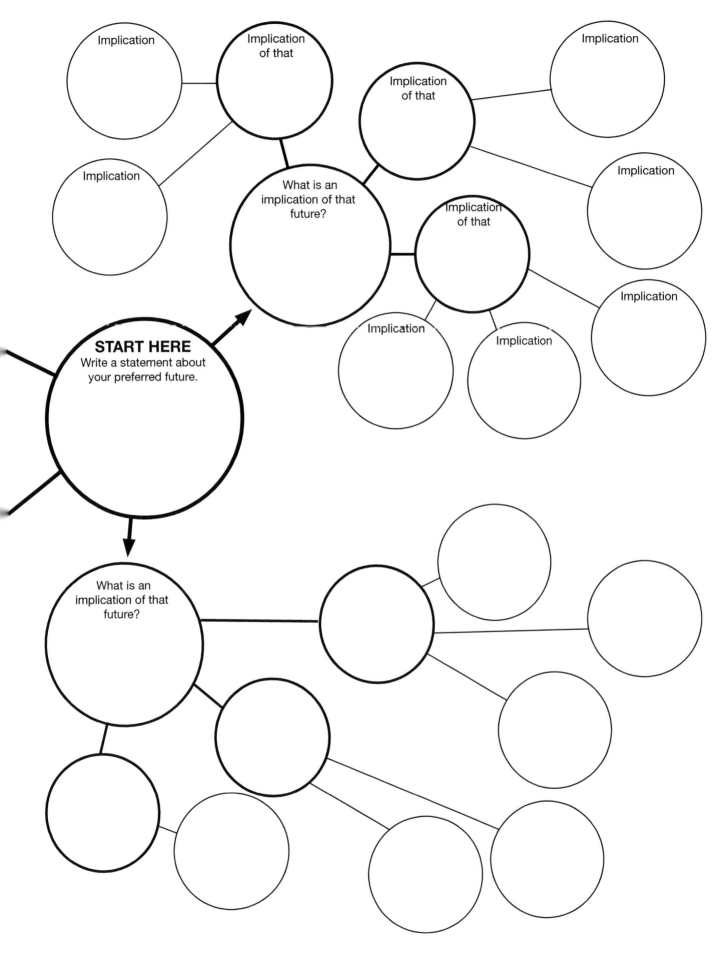

Final thoughts...

Before you move on to futures of your own making, capture your most impactful moments from this experience.

BIGGEST DISCOVERY
What did you discover about your futures that left the biggest impression?

BIGGEST CONSIDERATION
What did these exercises uncover that will need more consideration?

BIGGEST DESIRE
What is it that you cannot wait to try, build or explore? What do you now feel the need to do that you haven't felt before?

Printed in Germany
by Amazon Distribution
GmbH, Leipzig

What the Foresight is one of those rare feats – it is well informed, easy to understand and broadly applicable. If you're looking to take that first step into futures thinking here's your road map.

Brian David Johnson, *Futurist and author of Science Fiction Prototyping*

Going through the exercises in What the Foresight helps you envision multiple possible futures and then choose the path that suits you best. It's a imaginative and useful tool for anyone who wants to expand their options and explore more paths.

Christopher Ireland, *Co-author of Rise of the DEO*

Foresight is an emerging skill that is becoming more visible and more common around the world – that is, among adults. Young people are not yet included in the discussion of the future these days, and it's their future more than ours! Almost no schools teach students how to anticipate and influence change, much less about the plausible futures that await them later in life. Now Draudt and West have provided us with What the Foresight, a clever, beautifully designed approach to the future for young and old alike. Thank you!

Peter C. Bishop, Ph.D. *Executive Director of Teach the Future, Inc. and co-author of Thinking About the Future*

Finally, methodologies leveraged by leading strategic foresight practitioners have been made accessible. If there is one thing to takeaway from What the Foresight, it's this: the future is for everyone. In the book, authors Alida Draudt and Julia West brilliantly break down the guiding principles of futures work in an easy to understand set of materials and activities that anyone can use to imagine their own futures. Read this book! The future is a cause worth fighting for.

Matthew Manos, *Founder and Managing Director of verynice. Creator of Models of Impact, author of Toward a Preemptive Social Enterprise and author of How to Give Half of Your Work Away for Free*

ISBN 9781537424866

What the Foresight is one of those rare feats – it is well informed, easy to understand and broadly applicable. If you're looking to take that first step into futures thinking here's your road map.
    Brian David Johnson, *Futurist and author of Science Fiction Prototyping*

Going through the exercises in What the Foresight helps you envision multiple possible futures and then choose the path that suits you best. It's a imaginative and useful tool for anyone who wants to expand their options and explore more paths.
    Christopher Ireland, *Co-author of Rise of the DEO*

Foresight is an emerging skill that is becoming more visible and more common around the world – that is, among adults. Young people are not yet included in the discussion of the future these days, and it's their future more than ours! Almost no schools teach students how to anticipate and influence change, much less about the plausible futures that await them later in life. Now Draudt and West have provided us with What the Foresight, a clever, beautifully designed approach to the future for young and old alike. Thank you!
    Peter C. Bishop, Ph.D. *Executive Director of Teach the Future, Inc. and co-author of Thinking About the Future*

Finally, methodologies leveraged by leading strategic foresight practitioners have been made accessible. If there is one thing to takeaway from What the Foresight, it's this: the future is for everyone. In the book, authors Alida Draudt and Julia West brilliantly break down the guiding principles of futures work in an easy to understand set of materials and activities that anyone can use to imagine their own futures. Read this book! The future is a cause worth fighting for.
    Matthew Manos, *Founder and Managing Director of verynice. Creator of Models of Impact, author of Toward a Preemptive Social Enterprise and author of How to Give Half of Your Work Away for Free*

Sun Salutations

Hatha Yoga Surya Namaskar Vinyasa

Paul Newman